122

SilverTip

The Electoral College

by Daniel R. Faust

Consultant: John Coleman
Professor of Political Science, University of Minnesota
Minneapolis, Minnesota

BEARPORT
PUBLISHING

Minneapolis, Minnesota

Credits

Cover and Title Page, © Vacclav/iStock; 3, © Dan Thornberg/Shutterstock; 5, © Pool/Getty; 7, © Chip Somodevilla /Getty; 9, © Anadolu Agency/Getty; 13, © HANS PENNINK/Getty; 15, © Gints Ivuskans/ Shutterstock; 17T, © Bettmann/Getty; 17B, © Mike Flippo/Shutterstock; 19T, © Paul R. Jones/ Shutterstock; 19B, © Ryan DeBerardinis/Shutterstock; 21, © Burlingham/Shutterstock; 23, © Joseph Sohm/Shutterstock; 25, © Matt Smith Photographer/Shutterstock; 27, © Prostock-studio/Shutterstock; 28TL, © lyovajan/Shutterstock; 28TR, © Serdar Duran/Shutterstock; 28BL, © Alexkava/Shutterstock; 28BR, © Dave scar/Shutterstock.

President: Jen Jenson
Director of Product Development: Spencer Brinker
Senior Editor: Allison Juda
Associate Editor: Charly Haley
Senior Designer: Colin O'Dea

Library of Congress Cataloging-in-Publication Data

Names: Faust, Daniel R., author.
Title: The electoral college / by Daniel R. Faust.
Description: SilverTip Books. | Minneapolis, Minnesota : Bearport
    Publishing Company, [2022] | Series: U.S. Government : need to know |
    Includes bibliographical references and index.
Identifiers: LCCN 2021034166 (print) | LCCN 2021034167 (ebook) | ISBN
    9781636915982 (Library Binding) | ISBN 9781636916057 (Paperback) | ISBN
    9781636916125 (eBook)
Subjects: LCSH: Electoral college—United States. | Elections—United
    States. | Voting—United States. | Politics, Practical—United States.
Classification: LCC JK529 .F38 2022 (print) | LCC JK529 (ebook) | DDC
    324.6/3—dc23
LC record available at https://lccn.loc.gov/2021034166
LC ebook record available at https://lccn.loc.gov/2021034167

For more information, write to Bearport Publishing, 5357 Penn Avenue South, Minneapolis, MN 55419. Printed in the United States of America.

Contents

Picking a President

Every four years, the president of the United States is chosen. Voting is a big part of being in a **democracy**. But picking the president isn't simple. The president is voted into power by the Electoral College.

The president and the vice president are officially chosen by the Electoral College. They are the only people in government who are picked this way.

Election Day and Beyond

Many people in government are chosen through direct election. The people vote on the first Tuesday after the first Monday in November. In most states, all U.S. citizens 18 or older can have their say. The person, or **candidate**, who gets the most votes wins.

In the United States, there are elections at least every two years. People vote for members of their local, state, and federal government. Voting for the president happens every four years.

Senators are voted into power through direct elections.

For the president and vice president, the election doesn't stop in November. A small group of people called **electors** vote in December. Each person gets one vote for the president and one for the vice president. The Electoral College has voters from each state and the District of Columbia.

The election is made official in January. Congress counts the electoral votes. They say who is the winner. The president and vice president start their terms shortly after that.

Electoral votes
are kept safe until
Congress counts them.

Creating the College

How are electors split up? States get electors based on the number of people who live there. Every state has at least three electoral voters. After that, the states with more people get more voters. In total, there are 538 electors.

Each state is allowed to pick their electors. In many states, people from the political parties choose electors.

Electors per State

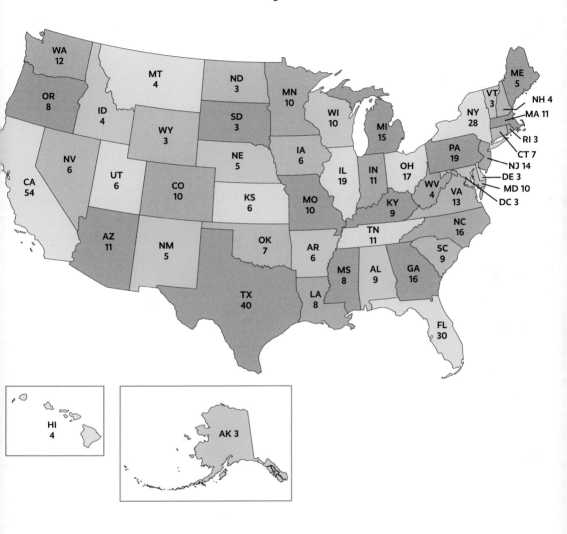

WA 12
MT 4
ND 3
MN 10
OR 8
ID 4
WY 3
SD 3
WI 10
MI 15
ME 5
VT 3
NH 4
NY 28
MA 11
NV 6
UT 6
CO 10
NE 5
IA 6
IL 19
IN 11
OH 17
PA 19
RI 3
CT 7
NJ 14
DE 3
MD 10
DC 3
CA 54
KS 6
MO 10
KY 9
WV 4
VA 13
AZ 11
NM 5
OK 7
AR 6
TN 11
NC 16
MS 8
AL 9
GA 16
SC 9
TX 40
LA 8
FL 30

HI 4
AK 3

The number of electors for each state may change every 10 years.

11

The Electoral Vote

Electors are supposed to vote the way people from their state voted. In most states, the candidate who wins the most votes from the people gets all of the state's electoral votes. It is called the winner-take-all system.

In Maine and Nebraska, electoral votes are split up. Each candidate gets votes based on how people from smaller areas, called districts, voted. Different electors from these states may vote for different people.

The president must win 270 Electoral College votes. But that's not always the whole story. The count of everyone's votes is called the popular vote. Sometimes the popular vote winners do not win the electoral votes. Even when this happens, the electoral vote winners become president and vice president.

Often, elections in winner-take-all states are close. But a candidate wins all the electoral votes for those states. So, they may win the election without the popular vote. Five presidents have not won the popular vote.

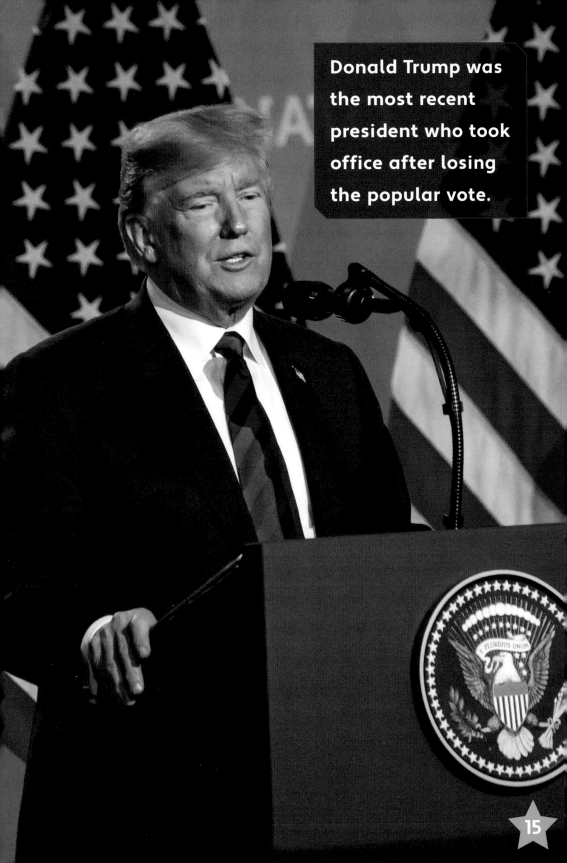

Donald Trump was the most recent president who took office after losing the popular vote.

An Old System

This system is old. It's almost as old as the United States. It was written into the Constitution. Some form of the college has been a part of every presidential election since the time of our first president, George Washington.

The Electoral College was a **compromise**. Some wanted to vote for the president and vice president in a direct election. Others wanted Congress to pick.

The United States was a new kind of government. The founders made the Electoral College.

The Best System?

It has been around for a long time. But is the Electoral College the best way to pick a president? Some people think so. They like how the college gives votes to smaller states. It gives power to places with fewer people. Otherwise, these people may not be heard.

People in different parts of the country might need different things from the government. For example, people with different jobs may want different laws.

Farmers usually live in places with fewer people. But the Electoral College still gives them a voice, just like businesspeople in crowded cities.

Some say the electoral college system needs to change. They think it gives too much power to the **majority**. The winner-take-all system may be to blame. It does not show how all the people from a state want to vote.

Some think the president should win by popular vote. They do not think it is right a candidate can win based on electoral votes instead.

People who vote the opposite way in winner-take-all states may not feel heard.

Changing the College

Some people want to get rid of the Electoral College. That would be hard to do. Still, some states have made changes to their voting systems. They will give their electoral votes to the candidate who wins the popular vote.

Changing the electoral college system would mean changing the Constitution. There have been only 27 changes, or amendments, to the Constitution in over 230 years.

Do the People's Votes Still Count?

The system may have problems. But is it completely broken? Does a single person's vote matter? The truth is that every vote counts. One vote can make a big difference. It can mean even more electoral votes go to a candidate.

Many states always vote for one political party over another. States that change with each election are called swing states. Just a few voters can make the whole state swing one way.

Presidential candidates spend a lot of time talking to voters in swing states.

Going Forward

Even people not in the college should vote. Electoral votes are made based on the choices of everyday voters. The president and vice president may be given their power by the Electoral College. But the decision comes from those who show up to vote in November.

Even those not old enough to vote can take a stand. Around the world, young people have made their voices heard. They may impact how adults vote.

How a President Is Elected

November Election
People across the country vote for the president and vice president.

Electoral College
Electors vote.

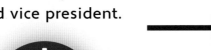

Congress Counts
Congress counts the electoral votes. The candidate with 270 votes or more wins.

Taking the Job
The president and vice president start their jobs on January 20.

★ SilverTips for REVIEW

Review what you've learned. Use the text to help you.

Define key terms

candidate

elector

popular vote

swing state

winner-take-all system

Check for understanding

Describe the steps needed for a candidate to be elected as president.

What is the difference between the popular vote and the electoral vote?

Name one reason people may like the Electoral College and one reason they may not.

Think deeper

How are the votes of the people important when it comes to electing a president of the United States?

★ SilverTips on TEST-TAKING

★ **Make a study plan.** Ask your teacher what the test is going to cover. Then, set aside time to study a little bit every day.

★ **Read all the questions carefully.** Be sure you know what is being asked.

★ **Skip any questions** you don't know how to answer right away. Mark them and come back later if you have time.

Glossary

candidate a person who is hoping for a job

compromise a way of reaching an agreement in which each side gives up something to find middle ground

Congress a part of the U.S. government that makes laws

democracy a form of government in which people choose leaders by voting

electors people who vote in the Electoral College to choose the president and vice president

federal having to do with the government of a nation

majority the group or party that is the larger number

political parties groups of people with similar values that join together to impact the policies of government

terms the time people serve in office

Read More

Hunt, Santana. *What Is the Electoral College? (A Look at Your Government).* New York: Gareth Stevens, 2018.

Meister, Cari. *The Electoral College: A Kid's Guide (Kids' Guide to Elections).* North Mankato, MN: Capstone Press, 2020.

Roosevelt, Eleanor, with Michelle Markel. *When You Grow Up to Vote: How Our Government Works for You.* New York: Roaring Brook Press, 2018.

Learn More Online

1. Go to **www.factsurfer.com** or scan the QR code below.

2. Enter "**Electoral College**" into the search box.

3. Click on the cover of this book to see a list of websites.

Index

About the Author

Daniel R. Faust is a freelance writer of fiction and nonfiction. He lives in Brooklyn, NY.